Exploring castles

Dr Brian Knapp

World history

Castles timeline

Norman rule (1066-1154)

1066   **1100**   **1200**

Normans
arrive

Tower of
London

William I 1066–1087 (The conqueror)
William II (Rufus) 1087–1100
Henry I (1100–1135)
Stephen 1135–1154

Henry II 1154–1189 (archbishop Becket murdered)
Richard (the lionheart) I 1189–1199 (Crusades)
(Bad) John 1199–1216 (Magna Carta 1215)
Henry III 1216–1272

Medieval times (11th–15th centuries)

0		**1000** AD		**2000** AD

Anglo-Saxons (450–1066)

Romans (700BC–476AD)

Vikings (800–1066/1400)

Tudors (1485–1603)

Victorians (1837–1901)

Contents

Look up the **bold** words in the glossary
on page 32 of this book.

House of Plantagenet (1154–1485)

Houses of Lancaster and York (1399–1485)

1300		**1400**		**1485**

Edward I (Longshanks) 1272–1307
Edward II 1307–1327
Edward III 1327–1377
Richard II 1377–1399

The Wars of the Roses (14th and 15th centuries)
House of Lancaster (1399–1471)
Henry IV 1399–1413
Henry V 1413–1422
Henry VI 1422–1461 and 1470–1471

House of York (1461–1485)
Edward VI 1461–1470
Edward IV 1471–1483
Edward V 1483
Richard III 1483–1485

Start of
Tudor times

Features of a castle

A castle was both a home and a fortress. Castles were built by rich and powerful people and guarded by their personal troops. So a castle was part home and part fort.

Castles were first built in the 11th century, when Norman (French) Duke William of Normandy (the Conqueror) became King William I of England after the Battle of Hastings in 1066.

William and his nobles were few in number and conquerors of a land that did not want them, so they had to protect themselves. To do this, they introduced the idea of a castle from Europe.

Did you know... ?

- Castle-building ended in the 15th century when the country became a safer place.
- Not all castles were built the same and their design changed over the centuries.
- The first (Norman) castles (picture right) had a tower (**keep**) on a mound (**motte**). There is also a tall wall (**curtain wall**).
- Castles built in later centuries (picture below) did not have a keep, but many giant towers and often two rings of walls.

Castles built in the 13th century and after usually did not have keeps. Instead, they had massive towers and walls.

Towers

Gatehouse with portcullis and drawbridge

Moat

Well

Curtain wall

Crenellated (embattled) top of wall (also called battlements)

Keep

Watchtower

Motte

Key to the ruins. (Only features common to most castles are shown.)

Q **Why did the Normans build castles?**

Motte and tower

The simplest thing to build is a stronghold – a house strengthened to protect it from attackers. If this building stands on its own it is called a tower house.

It needs to have thick walls so it cannot be knocked down by attackers. It should not have an entrance at ground level, for that would make it too easy to enter. It should only have slits for windows so that people inside could not be shot. It should have a lead roof so that fire arrows would do no harm.

The motte and keep at Cardiff castle. This is a very simple design of keep, and archers could not see along all of the walls to keep off attackers.

The Clifford tower in York is a keep on a motte.

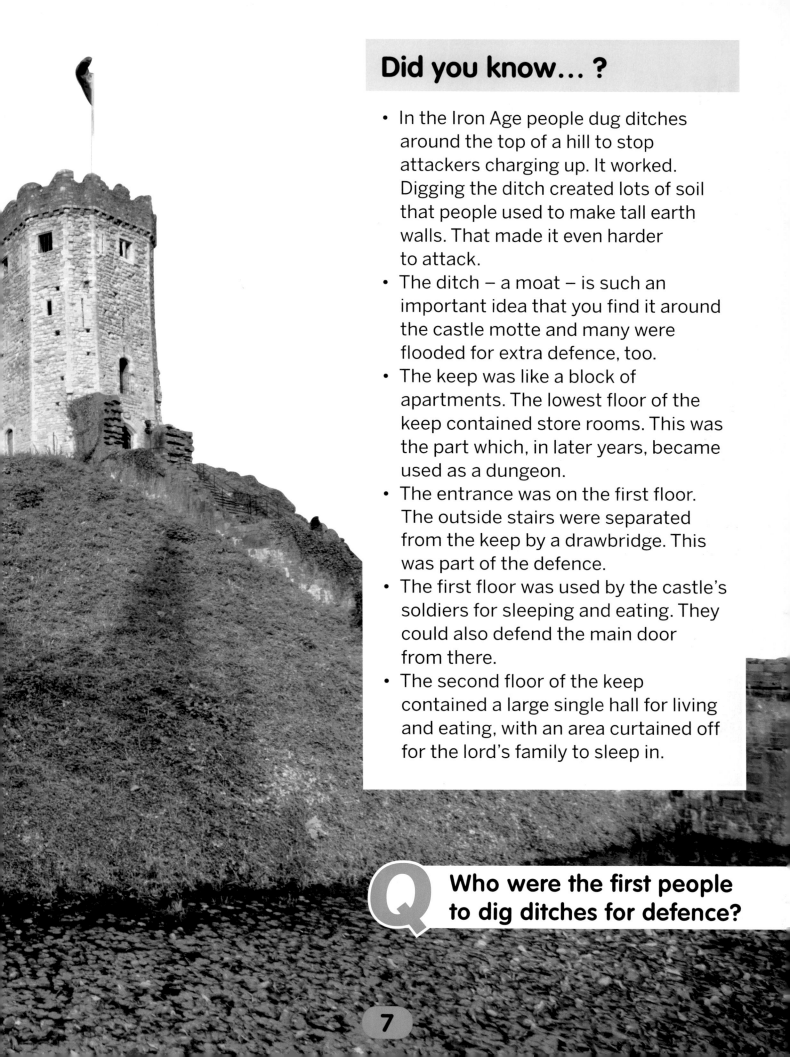

Did you know... ?

- In the Iron Age people dug ditches around the top of a hill to stop attackers charging up. It worked. Digging the ditch created lots of soil that people used to make tall earth walls. That made it even harder to attack.
- The ditch – a moat – is such an important idea that you find it around the castle motte and many were flooded for extra defence, too.
- The keep was like a block of apartments. The lowest floor of the keep contained store rooms. This was the part which, in later years, became used as a dungeon.
- The entrance was on the first floor. The outside stairs were separated from the keep by a drawbridge. This was part of the defence.
- The first floor was used by the castle's soldiers for sleeping and eating. They could also defend the main door from there.
- The second floor of the keep contained a large single hall for living and eating, with an area curtained off for the lord's family to sleep in.

Q Who were the first people to dig ditches for defence?

Wall

A tower on a mound is not ideal. For example, the soldiers who helped to protect the castle had nowhere for their horses. Castles needed space for workers, such as blacksmiths, saddlers and other tradesmen to do their work. The castle wall was built to give them a place to do this, as well as being a strong barrier against attackers.

Soldiers on horseback are called cavalry.

Crenellations (battlements)

Tall watchtowers to spot attack, and to allow shooting over the walls

Towers that stand away from the wall and allow archers to fire at attackers trying to scale the walls

The number of towers depended on the size of the wall. An attacker must come under fire from two towers at the same time, so they could not be too far apart. This is Caernarfon castle.

Did you know... ?

- The wall was many metres thick.
- It was not made of solid stone, but had faces of stone blocks and an inside of rubble. It was much cheaper and easier to build that way.
- The top had special places where archers could fire down. The tops of the walls are called the battlements. The protected sections were usually twice as wide as the firing sections. The up and down pattern is called **crenellation**. The cut-out part is called a crenel, the upstanding part is called a merlon.
- The wall was protected by towers along its length. Towers jutted out beyond the line of the wall so that archers in the towers could shoot along the line of the wall at attackers.
- A nobleman had to ask the king for permission to build like this. It was called a 'licence to crenellate'.

The inside of the wall had stairs and there was a walkway all around the top. Archers stood behind the merlons and fired through the crenels.

Q How did soldiers get to the top of the wall?

Arrow loops

Gatehouse

A wall with no openings is very hard to break down. But then no-one can get out, either. So every wall had a gate.

The gate could be the weakest spot – a place where battering rams could do damage. So great care was taken to protect the gate. In many cases huge towers were placed alongside the gate to make a gatehouse.

The gate was made very narrow so it could not be charged, and protected by iron grills that could be let down into it. These were **portcullises**. Some castles had several portcullises. The gate was further protected with a **drawbridge** over the moat.

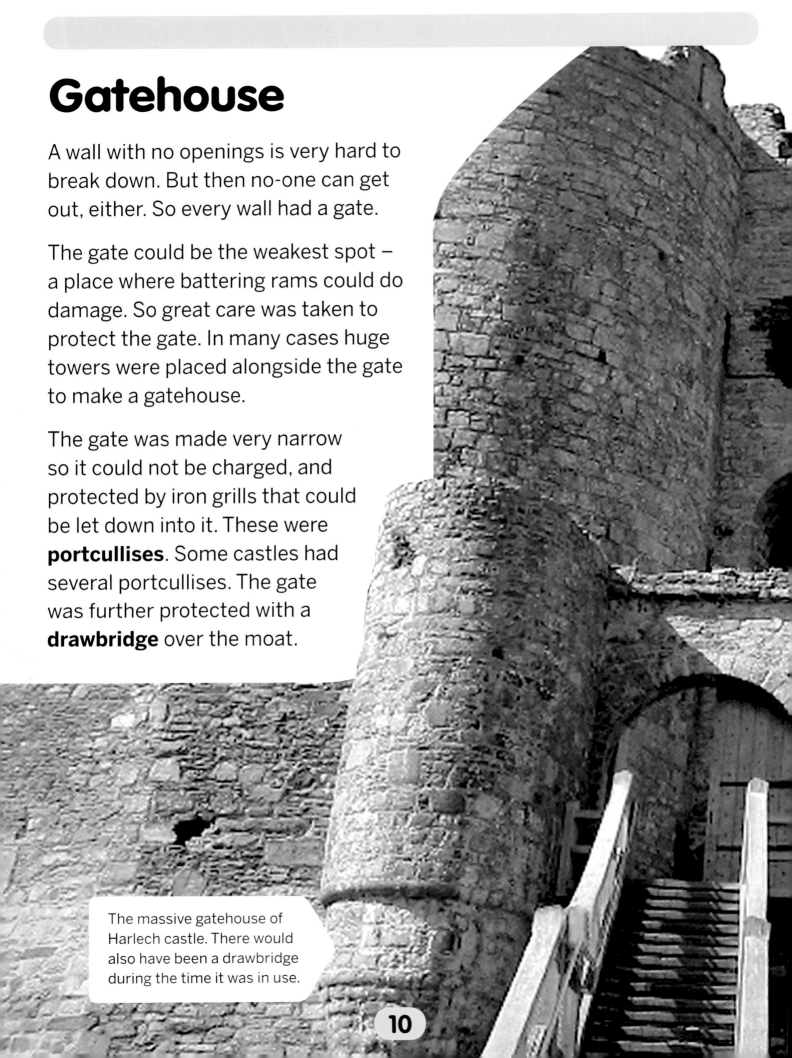

The massive gatehouse of Harlech castle. There would also have been a drawbridge during the time it was in use.

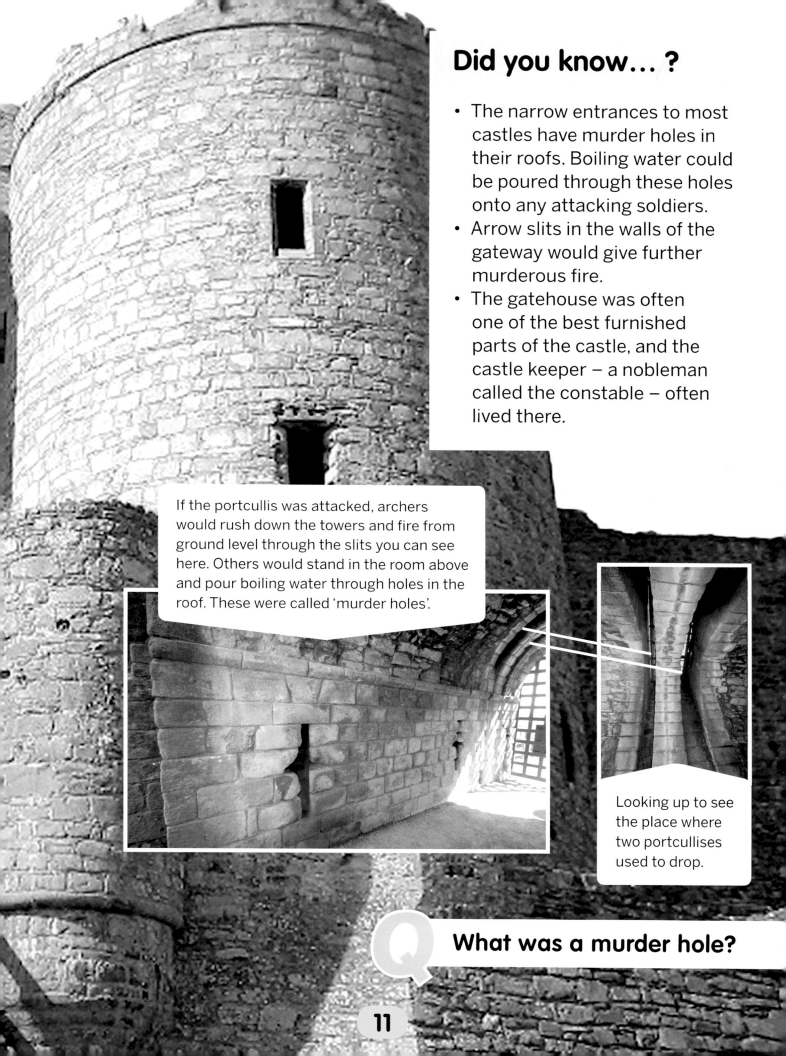

Did you know…?

- The narrow entrances to most castles have murder holes in their roofs. Boiling water could be poured through these holes onto any attacking soldiers.
- Arrow slits in the walls of the gateway would give further murderous fire.
- The gatehouse was often one of the best furnished parts of the castle, and the castle keeper – a nobleman called the constable – often lived there.

If the portcullis was attacked, archers would rush down the towers and fire from ground level through the slits you can see here. Others would stand in the room above and pour boiling water through holes in the roof. These were called 'murder holes'.

Looking up to see the place where two portcullises used to drop.

What was a murder hole?

Getting about in a castle

A castle had to keep those who lived inside safe from attack. This is why castles had thick stone walls. In fact, the walls were not just thick, they were very, very thick – usually several metres.

The walls were thick enough to have stairs and corridors built inside them. This made it more comfortable to get about in the cold of winter, and very much safer if the castle was being attacked.

Castle keeps were built with the entrance on the first floor. There was no entrance on the ground floor. This meant that an attacker had to climb stairs to get to the front entrance, and so was more easily beaten back. The higher up you went, the safer it was – at least for a while – and so the rooms used by the lord and lady were on the first and second floors. In some towers the bedrooms were on higher floors still.

Did you know… ?

- Spiral stairs nearly always spiral to the right as most people are right handed. If an attacker was racing up the stairs with sword in hand, he could not wield the sword while going up a right-handed spiral. The defender, on the other hand, had his right hand in the clear.
- The entrance to the **great hall**, where the lord held court and met guests, was reached by a grand staircase.
- The stairs down to where the food and drink were kept – buttery, pantry, wine and beer cellars – were not used by the lord and so were of lower quality.
- Stairs within the walls were very dark, with perhaps only the odd window slit for light.

Often the only straight stairs were between the entrance to the great hall and the kitchens.

Q Why do stairs spiral to the right?

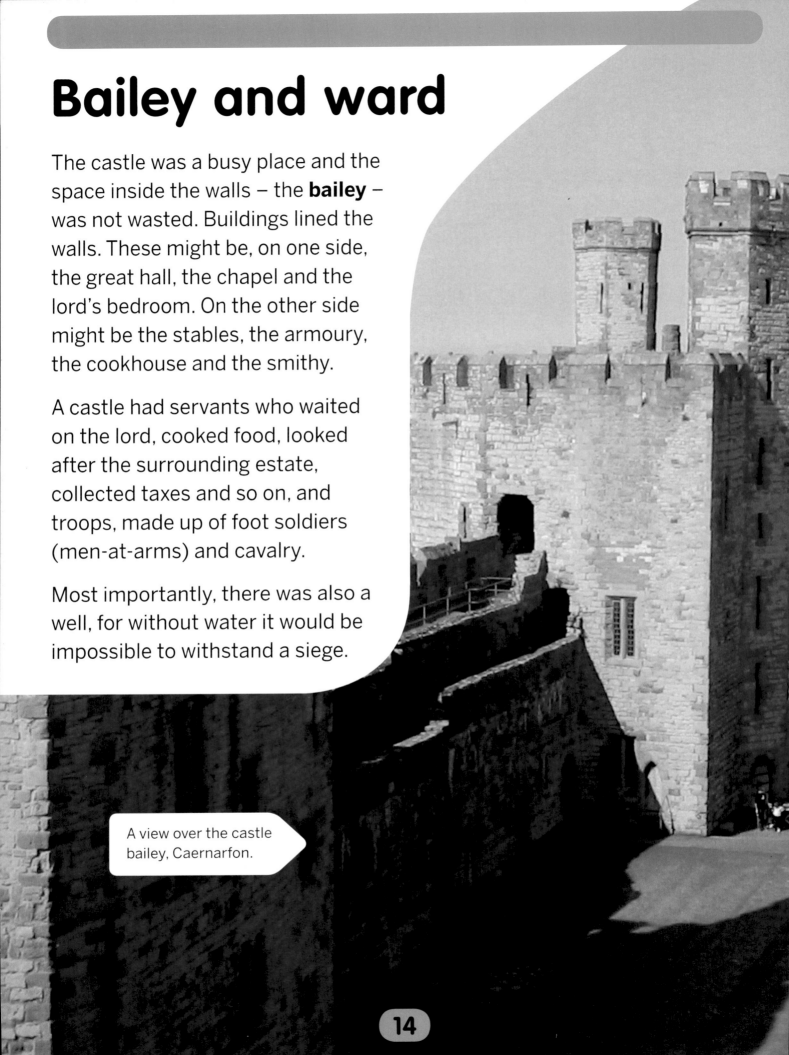

Bailey and ward

The castle was a busy place and the space inside the walls – the **bailey** – was not wasted. Buildings lined the walls. These might be, on one side, the great hall, the chapel and the lord's bedroom. On the other side might be the stables, the armoury, the cookhouse and the smithy.

A castle had servants who waited on the lord, cooked food, looked after the surrounding estate, collected taxes and so on, and troops, made up of foot soldiers (men-at-arms) and cavalry.

Most importantly, there was also a well, for without water it would be impossible to withstand a siege.

A view over the castle bailey, Caernarfon.

Did you know… ?

- Many castles had two sets of walls. The inner walls were higher than the outer walls so archers on the inner walls could fire over the heads of those on the outer walls.
- If the area inside the wall was complicated, the parts were often called wards, for example, outer ward and inner ward.

Q **What was the bailey used for?**

Ward/bailey

Where were castles built?

Castles had to be built in places that were easy to defend. If possible, castles were built on high ground. Edinburgh castle is built on a crag of hard rock that is almost impossible to climb. Otherwise they chose places such as the narrow neck of a river loop. The loop (meander) of the river was a natural moat and the castle simply had to defend a narrow neck of land.

Edinburgh castle on its craggy hill.

What the castle and village or town might have looked like in medieval times.

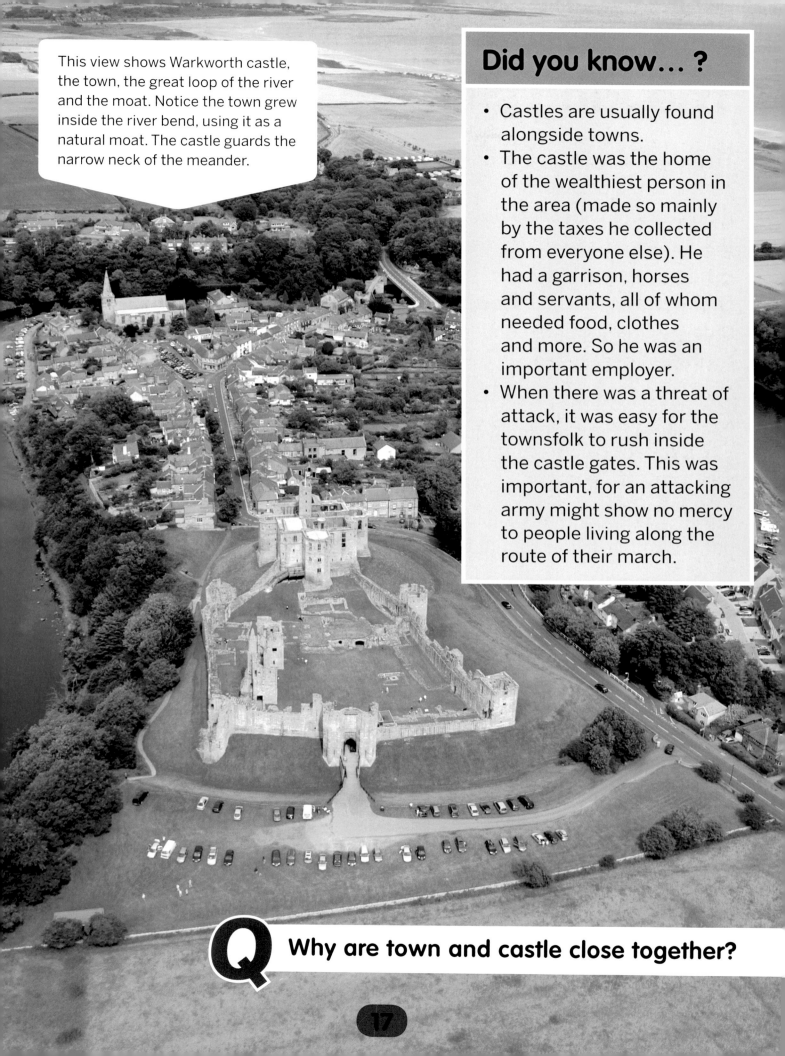

This view shows Warkworth castle, the town, the great loop of the river and the moat. Notice the town grew inside the river bend, using it as a natural moat. The castle guards the narrow neck of the meander.

Did you know... ?

- Castles are usually found alongside towns.
- The castle was the home of the wealthiest person in the area (made so mainly by the taxes he collected from everyone else). He had a garrison, horses and servants, all of whom needed food, clothes and more. So he was an important employer.
- When there was a threat of attack, it was easy for the townsfolk to rush inside the castle gates. This was important, for an attacking army might show no mercy to people living along the route of their march.

Q Why are town and castle close together?

The king's castles

The Tower of London was built in the corner of the old Roman fort. At that time everything between the sea and the castle was marshy, so the Tower of London guarded the River Thames. The river was also much shallower than it is today, so the Tower of London guarded the river crossing, too.

The Tower was one of the first castles to be built, so it was originally just a keep, known as the White Tower. It was built on a motte. But as it was so important, its defences could not be allowed to go out of fashion. It was rebuilt time after time. This is why it is now surrounded by a double wall as well. Windsor did not need as much protection and so it only has a single wall.

The Tower of London has a double curtain wall with many towers on the inner wall.

ENTRY TO THE TRAITORS GATE

The White Tower.

Did you know…?

- The central keep of the Tower of London was begun in 1078, just twelve years after the Norman conquest of England.
- William ordered the Tower to be built of white limestone brought from his native city of Caen in Normandy. The tower was finished in 1087.
- In 1240 Henry III had the tower whitewashed, which is how it became known as the White Tower.
- Its walls are up to 5 m thick and rise 27 m from the ground.

Windsor castle is Britain's biggest castle and is on high land guarding the route along the River Thames. It has a keep with two baileys and a curtain wall. The royal chapel and other public areas are on the left, the royal apartments are on the right. It was used as a royal 'holiday-home'.

Q **Why is the keep of the Tower of London called the 'White Tower'?**

How castles were destroyed

There were many ways to attack a castle. The most common tactic was a **siege**. The enemy would surround a castle and not allow food in or people out.

A siege was very unpleasant. As food ran low, women and children were forced out of the castle since they were no help in defending it and they ate valuable rations.

The attackers and defenders knew the rules of the game. If the constable (the castle manager) could see there was no chance of winning, he would surrender and come out with colours flying and suffer no disgrace. Things only got nasty if the defenders decided to stay and defend.

When a castle was attacked the gate could be hammered with a battering ram. A siege engine, an armoured tower, could be wheeled alongside the walls so that soldiers could walk across to the battlements. Giant catapults threw stones, fireballs, dead animals, and even plague victims, over the walls.

The favourite tactic was to dig a tunnel under the castle walls or tower, then set the supporting tunnel woodwork alight. The heavy wall or tower would then collapse.

This is what a battering ram looked like. The roof gave protection to the troops.

Did you know…?

- During the reign of horrid John 1 (1199–1216) the barons staged a revolt. A group of barons rushed to the port of Rochester on the River Medway in Kent and seized control of the castle. John decided to take the castle by force. Five siege engines were built against the castle walls and a tunnel dug under the wall. By early November, 1215, the king's men had got through the wall and began tunnelling under the keep. This caused the whole corner of the keep to fall down. Some rebels surrendered and left the castle but, on John's orders, had their hands and feet cut off.
- The castle was finally taken on 30th November by starvation and not by force.
- The fallen tower was rebuilt as a round tower as this is better for defence. See it in this picture.

Attackers might use all kinds of towers to allow their men to get to the top of the walls. This tower is called a belfry.

Q **What was a siege engine for?**

All the comforts of home...

In the early days of castles, the fire was in the centre of the hall, and hot, smoky air had to find its own way out. Then fireplaces were invented and set inside the walls. There were even chimney pots on the roof. Kitchens were built into the lower floors of the keep.

In the earliest castles, everyone 'did their business' on the floor of the hall or outside. It was all cleared away a few times a year. By the 14th century the lord and lady, and some of the high officials, each had their own sitting room, bedroom and loo (**garderobe**) – in fact, they had en-suite living.

Massive fireplaces were needed to cook for the castle staff. Great fires would have been fitted with cauldrons for the stew (potage) most people ate, and the roasting spits for the game the lord enjoyed.

A garderobe.

Garderobe (toilet) tower with ventilation windows

Waste falls down tower chute

Outflow

Stone seat (now protected by an iron grille).

Looking up the garderobe tower to the toilet seat.

How did a garderobe make life better?

The great hall

The hall was the most important room in the castle. In keeps the hall was on the first floor. In later castles it was a large room built against an inner castle wall. In both cases, the hall was where the lord and his family ate and saw visitors.

The lord and lady sat to eat on a raised platform at one end, while everyone else would sit on benches. In early keeps the benches would be cleared away at night and a curtain drawn across the raised area. The lord and his family would then sleep with a small amount of privacy. Everyone else slept on the main floor. Beds were not common except for the wealthiest people.

Things improved over the centuries. By the 14th century most windows were glazed. Nobles had their own living apartments built next to the hall.

Most people went to bed early, but from time to time, entertainment would be laid on. This would have

A great hall with painted wall decoration and a large fireplace. (The furniture is more recent.)

included minstrels, jesters and troubadours.

Most castle troops and workers ate bread. They did not get meat very often. When they did get to eat meat it was usually fish. Their bread was dipped in a stew called potage, which was usually made of vegetables. For entertainment, the castle staff might sing songs and tell stories while gathered around a fire in the bailey.

Did you know... ?

- Many halls had a minstrel gallery where players would entertain while the diners ate.
- A large window faced out on to the bailey.
- The passageway next to this table would lead to the lord's private apartments.
- Most great halls also had a large fireplace as this was the main living room of the castle.
- There were tapestries on the walls.
- Medieval chefs liked to flavour the food, partly because then you couldn't taste that it might be well past its 'sell-by' date and would otherwise smell.
- Most people ate with their knives and a wooden spoon. Forks had not been invented. Most plates (platters) were of wood, as were many goblets.

Q **Why did they have rushes on the floor?**

The floor in this picture is cleaner than it would have been in the 15th century. The floor would have been strewn with rushes. It was common for people to 'relieve themselves' without leaving the room. Also when people had finished their food, they simply tipped the remains, such as bones, on the floor. Mixing herbs with the rushes helped keep down the smell until the rushes were swept away and new ones laid (which was not very often).

Fighting

Castles were not home to thousands of armed men. No-one could afford the cost. Most castles only had a few tens of cavalry and perhaps a few dozen more men-at-arms.

If a major battle was fought, armies were made up by taking a few dozen from the garrison in each castle along the marching route, and by commanding peasants on each estate to leave their fields and join the army.

Reconstruction fight with long, two-handed swords that could be used for slashing down on footsoldiers and also in hand-to-hand fighting, after the horsemen had dismounted.

Protective helmet.

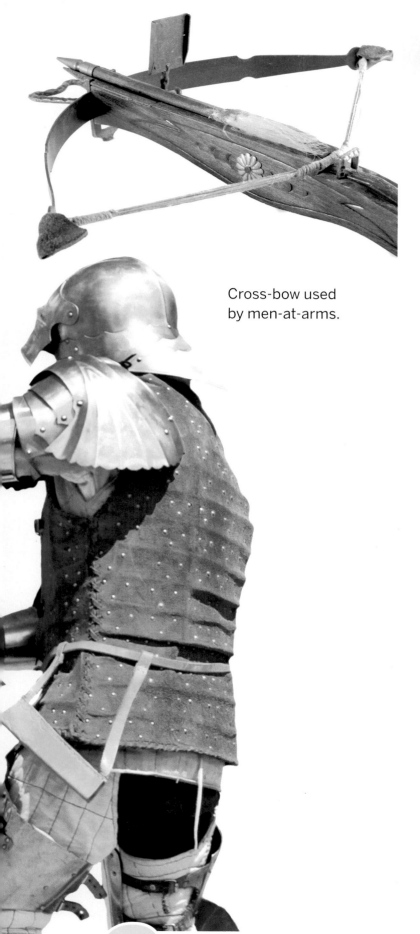

Cross-bow used by men-at-arms.

Did you know… ?

- The lord had to trust his soldiers because he didn't want them turning against him. Part of this trust came through a code of conduct called **chivalry**.
- The French word for knight is chevalier (person skilled in the ways of a horse, after the French word 'cheval'). The word cavalry comes from the same source.
- There were two kinds of mounted soldier: cavalrymen, who were mounted soldiers paid by the lord and just lightly armoured. Then there were the knights, who were much more heavily armoured and used only in times of great need.
- The knight was originally a riding servant of the king. Over the centuries knights believed they should protect all of the weak (especially fair maidens) and churches, as well as the Christian religion.
- If you were a knight and taken prisoner you were looked after well while someone went to find the money to ransom you. If you were a cavalryman, or a foot soldier, you would simply be slaughtered, as no code of chivalry applied to you, and you were not going to be worth ransoming either.

Q **What were the weapons used by medieval troops?**

Tournaments and jousting

It's hard to find space inside the castle walls to keep fit and show off your strength. As a result, special areas were set aside outside the walls. But knights were interested in competing, so they often travelled to other castles to take part in sporting events. These were costly and only usually offered by the wealthiest nobles.

In early medieval times knights took part in tournaments. There were mock battles. Two sides fought it out by means of a horseback charge using lances held level. The idea was to knock someone off their horse, ride on, turn and ride back into the fight to knock another opponent off their horse. It got very wild and was eventually banned.

Jousting was where two knights rode at each other. Over time, jousting became the main event for knights to show off their skill.

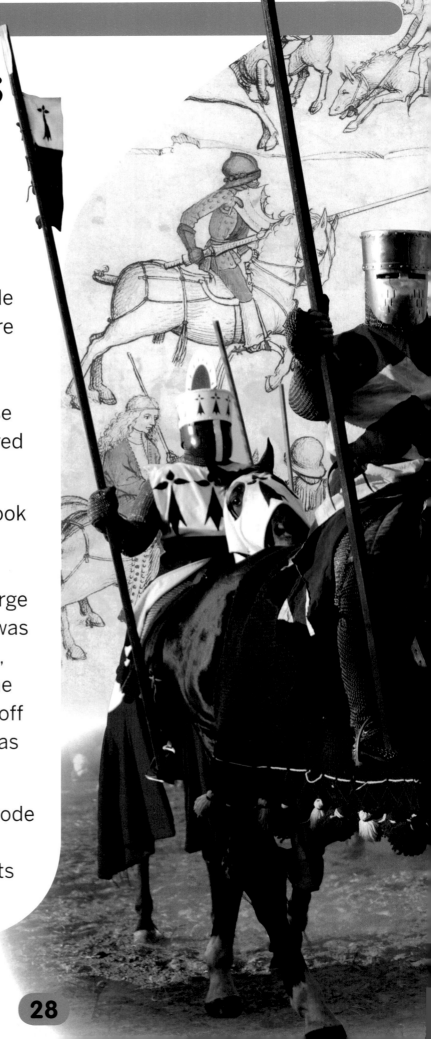

A tournament as shown in a medieval book.

Did you know... ?

- The word tournament is French, meaning turning around.
- Only early knights wore rings of iron meshed together and called **chain mail**.
- In later medieval times the fashion changed to plate armour.
- Plate armour was often so heavy the rider had to be lifted up on his horse with the help of his squire, and the horse he rode had to be more like a cart horse.
- Lances for jousting were made of solid oak.
- In jousting, horses did not gallop (and probably could not under such a weight), but simply cantered, so there was time for the riders to plan their thrust. Knights did not run full pelt at the opponent, for that increased the chances of missing the target.

Reconstruction, showing colour patterns for identification (coats of arms, etc).

Reconstruction of jousting.

What was a coat of arms for?

29

Why are castles now in ruins?

Just like any house, castles needed to be maintained, or the roof would leak, the walls would lose their cement and so on. So it had to be so important to have a castle that all of the costs were worth it.

By the end of Medieval times, nobles felt safer – unless they rebelled against the king or queen. There were also better and more comfortable ways of living. So nobles built themselves stately homes and let their castles fall to wrack and ruin.

In the 17th century Civil War, the time when the king and Parliament were fighting one another, the king's supporters often stayed in castles. When the Parliamentary forces took the castles – by firing cannon at the walls – they then pulled most of the remaining walls down and took the gates away so they could not be used for defence any more.

Did you know… ?

- The outside of castle walls are made of good stone that could be stolen and reused for new houses.
- The roof was clad in lead, which could be sold.
- The roof beams were good oak, which could be reused.
- Moats fill in unless they are regularly dredged.
- In the 19th century, some penniless lords actually sold off their own castle remains to make money.
- Only the wealthiest families kept their castles as going concerns and that is why so few survive today.

Glossary

BAILEY The area inside the curtain wall.

CHAIN MAIL Flexible armour made of iron links. A shirt made from mail is a hauberk.

CHIVALRY The way that medieval knights fought to a set of well-defined rules.

CRENELLATION The pattern of alternating higher and lower tops to the walls of many medieval castles. Also known as battlements.

CURTAIN WALL The main outer wall of the castle.

DRAWBRIDGE A bridge over a moat that could be lifted to stop attackers reaching the castle gate.

GARDEROBE A very simple toilet set in a small private room in a castle wall.

GREAT HALL The main living area of the castle owner and the place where business was conducted.

KEEP The central tower of an early castle.

MOAT The ditch around a castle used to help protection. Many, but not all, moats had water in.

MOTTE The mound of earth on which the keep was built.

PORTCULLIS A metal grille that could be lowered to block the route through the gatehouse.

SIEGE A way of attacking a castle by surrounding it and trying to starve the defenders out.

Index

Curriculum Visions

Curriculum Visions Explorers

This series provides straightforward introductions to key worlds and ideas.

You might also be interested in

Our slightly more detailed 48 pp book, 'A castle home'. All of our products are suitable for KS2.

Dedicated Web Site

Watch movies, see many more pictures and read much more in detail about dinosaurs and other topics:

www.curriculumvisions.com

(It's my turn! and the Learning Centre are subscription areas of the web site)

A CVP Book
Copyright © 2010 Atlantic Europe Publishing

Author
Brian Knapp, BSc, PhD

Senior Designer
Adele Humphries, BA

Editor
Gillian Gatehouse

Photographs
The Earthscape and Shutterstock Picture Libraries, except the following: (c=centre t=top b=bottom l=left r=right) *Wikipedia* page 18bl, 19br, 20br, 28–29.

Designed and produced by
Atlantic Europe Publishing

Printed in China by
WKT Company Ltd

Exploring castles
– *Curriculum Visions*
A CIP record for this book is available from the British Library
ISBN 978 1 86214 611 2

This product is manufactured from sustainable managed forests. For every tree cut down at least one more is planted.